THE LONGEST NIGHT

THE LONGEST NIGHT

A collection of poetry from a life half lived.

RANATA SUZUKI

ILLUSTRATIONS BY SEAMLESS

THE LONGEST NIGHT

First Printing: 2018

ISBN 978 0 646 98740 8

www.ranatasuzuki.com

DEDICATION

"No words exist to accurately describe the infinite ways in which your soul touches mine. If they did, I would surely have written them by now.

And yet, I continue to write."

CONTENTS

A PARALLEL UNIVERSE

There was a time in my life not so long ago, in which I
experienced a moment that could only be described as pure love
and happiness.

It was as if love and happiness were finally real to me
and they were something tangible, embodied in that moment.
They were in everything I could hear, touch, taste and smell. I
could see them with my very eyes, reflected back at me in
someone else's. They were all around me, breathing life into me
as if wrapping me up in a divine blanket.

And in that moment I caught a glimpse of something – a
parallel universe, a way things could have been – an alternate
reality where that love and happiness were mine to keep, a place
where I didn't have to let them go.

I only hope that one day, many years from now, when
this delicate thread of life has been pulled until its end and I close
my weary eyes for the last and final time, I will open them again
… and find myself there.

When
do you let the bird go?

CHAPTER 1
SUNSET

*'I've never been the most important thing to anybody
– not even myself.'*

FATE

He would fill me with butterflies – delicate and beautiful
flutterings that would dance into life whenever he was near.
Perhaps he took them with him when he left?
Or maybe it was fate.
Butterflies never live very long.

THE WEARY TRAVELLER

You were a road stop on my journey, that's what I keep telling
myself.
Some out-of-the-way oasis I stumbled upon at a point in my life
I was so tired, I honestly didn't want to go on any more.
You felt like an adventure, yet you felt like home.
Every new aspect of you I uncovered felt intriguing yet familiar,
like I had explored you before in some long forgotten dream.
You were a place I could have stayed forever ... a place I didn't
want to leave behind.
A place I will always be grateful for, whose name I will never
forget, and that I will search for in my travels for the rest of my
days whilst knowing in my heart I will never find it again.

You were a road stop on my journey ... that's what I keep telling
myself.

I just wish you'd been the destination.

A FAIRYTALE

Every quote, every book, every film seemed to suggest that
'one day' someone would come into my life and love me with
an intensity and a passion I had never experienced before.
And to their credit they were right; it all came and went so fast,
it really did feel as if it were just one day.

A LETTER TO THE SUN
FROM THE DARK SIDE OF THE MOON

To my dearest love
        my brilliant Sun,
the world has decided
        we can no longer be one.

So you take the day
        and I'll take the night,
you with your warm, happy glow
        me with my cold, lonely light.

It must be this way,
        always and forever,
they say we can no longer
        share the sky together.

But my nights will follow
        your brilliant days,
I am right behind you
        and I will love you always.

So do not be sad my love
        please do not fret,
for my reason to rise
        is in watching you set.

So never forget
        that there once was a time,
when I truly was yours
        and you truly were mine.

That there once was a moment
        when I felt you lips …
if ever you miss me
        remember our eclipse.

THE DESCENT

I ran	out of reasons to be cautious of you.
I walked	the fine line between friendship and love.
I stood	on the edge, knowing the next step could
	never be undone.
I fell	for you … harder than I ever dreamed possible.
I lay down	with you, loved you, opened myself to you.
I gave up	my defences, cast aside all my masks.
I died	a thousand times in the thousand lives
	I dreamed within your eyes.
	Not one was lived …
without you.	

SHATTERED GLASS

Have you ever loved someone who makes you feel like you
are glass?
Fragile and delicate, but also transparent; like there's nothing
within you they cannot see.
It's an unnerving yet beautiful feeling ... until they shatter you.

LOVES REASON

I didn't love you to seek revenge.
I didn't love you out of loneliness or unhappiness.
I didn't love you for any of the misguided reasons that time might convince you I did.

I just loved you because you were you.

STALEMATE

Our parting was like a stalemate.
Neither of us won, yet both of us lost.
And worse still ... that unshakable feeling that nothing was ever
really finished.

WHEN DO YOU LET THE BIRD GO?

It is my belief
that a caged bird is a cruelty
and that if you love something
more than you love yourself
you set it free.

But my heart was not
the only fluttering thing in that breath-held moment
as I reached out
with feather-light touch and nervous hand
disquieted by the piercing screech
of a cage door opening.

Mine was not
the only sharp intake of breath
in that moment of betrayal
when it shot from the cage
like a sniper's bullet to my heart
never once looking back.

And the question on my mind
now it is done and my bird set free
the thing I so desperately wish to know …
when do you let the bird go?

Is it that moment
with eyes straining and light fading
you watch as its last trace is forever sacrificed to the horizon?
Or is it the day, many years since
when hope fades with the light
and you finally stop looking at the horizon
waiting for it to come back.

Will it be
a slow cancerous process
the gritty pain of a cage door rusted open
just so it will never hold another bird again.
Or will it be
a sudden change
like a wind of regret carrying on it both a stray feather
and the realisation that tears are the only thing to ever come back.

Will it be
a fortitude gained with time
when I no longer seek its tune
in every melody I hear?
Or will it be
painfully stripped away
layer by layer
years – like vultures
slowly picking off one by one
every subtle nuance of its voice
until the memory's bleached bones
are all that are left.

Or perhaps it is all an illusion
created by the heart
an ever-spinning thaumatrope
in which the captor is the bird
and sorrow the cage –
for the door is open, yet you cannot leave.
You are never truly free until you let the bird go,
and when will that be?

Please tell me,
for I would dearly love to know ...

When do you let the bird go?

THE FOOLISH GIRL

And what a foolish girl you were,
to put your heart in the lion's mouth,
then cry when he swallowed you whole.

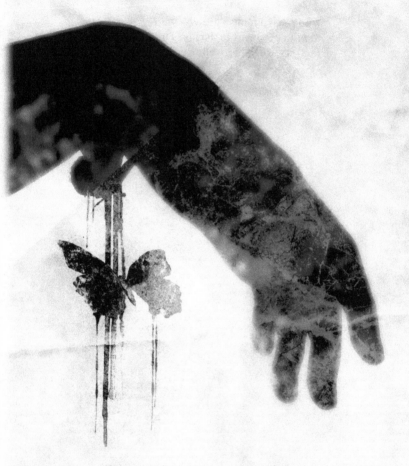

Or maybe it was fate...
        butterflies never live very long.

CHAPTER 2
DARKNESS

'There comes a point where you no longer care if there's a light at the end of the tunnel or not. You're just sick of the tunnel.'

CAUSE OF DEATH

He looked at my clothes and said, *'There is no need to hide anything from me. Show me everything. Take them off for me and I will love all of you just as you are.'*
So I took off my clothes, and true to his word, he loved all of me just as I was.

He looked at my skin and said, *'There is no need to hold everything inside so tightly. Bleeding is not a weakness. Open up for me and I will hold you together.'*
So from my throat to my naval, I cut open my skin, and true to his word, he held me together.

He looked at my ribs and said, *'There is no need to keep what is tender inside that protective cage. Learn to trust. Let the cage swing open for me and I will guard what is sensitive within you.'*
So I broke open my ribcage, and true to his word, he protected all that was fragile inside me.

He looked at my insides and said, *'There is no need to do everything alone. Share the burden. Give me all that is inside you, as I will be everything that keeps you alive.'*
So I gave him my all. My heart, my lungs – everything I had inside me to give ... and true to his word, he was in my every breath and heartbeat.

And so I lay with him, dissected to my very core. I had opened myself to him, given him every part of myself I had to offer. No longer soulless automated responses, we existed as one. He was my soulmate, my other half, his blood through my veins, my breath in his lungs.

Then he looked into my eyes and said, *'Goodbye ...'*
And suddenly I lay alone.

My chest ripped open; I was completely hollowed out and empty inside.
The bottomless pit of my torso felt only intense chilling pain, like a tooth cavity exposed to the cold air.
Without him, I was naked and exposed.
My heart had no one to beat for.
I couldn't breathe without him.

The irony is that only the living can die.
He brought me to life ... and now I am an empty cadaver that any first-year med student could peer at and say with solemn certainty, *'The cause of death ... was life'*.

THE FIVE STAGES OF GRIEF

When you experience loss, people say you'll move through
the five stages of grief:
Denial
Anger
Bargaining
Depression
Acceptance

What they don't tell you is that you'll cycle through them all
– every, single day.

SHE WEARS IT WELL

She wears it so beautifully doesn't she, her pain – always smiling,
always positive, always happy to help.
It's like a garment perfectly tailored to fit the way she carries it,
with a touch of grace and the quietness of that sad smile ...

All so you'd never know how heavy it really was.

HEART OF HEARTS

I know what you want in your heart of hearts.
You want me to be happy.
You want me to move on with my life …
but not too much.
Because you want to run into me one day and be able to talk about old times.
You want me to laugh with you, smile and say, *'Yeah … it was really something'*.

And I can't …
because it was everything.

THE VISITOR

It's true you felt like home to me – but not my own home.
No, you felt like other people's houses did when I was
growing up – pleasant, and normal ... and safe.
Not perfect, but full of love – the kind of love I'd always
wanted ...
The kind of love I would linger in for as long as possible before
ultimately I had to leave because I knew it wasn't mine.
I didn't belong there ... I was just a visitor.

LOVE LIKE DROWNING

I believe it is entirely possible to love somebody too much.
To give so much of yourself that you find you are almost empty
with nothing but a longing to fill yourself with thoughts of them.
Make no mistake, love can be a destructive force ... it can
consume you to the point of imbalance.
You can give so much of yourself away and take on so much of
someone else that you become like a boat taking on water ...
I believe you can drown in a person if you let yourself.
You can think them, breathe them, you can want to become part
of them so badly that it's almost as if you no longer exist.
You become them – their desires are yours.
Their hopes, their aspirations and their dreams become yours.
You exist solely as an extension of them.
You become utterly and completely absorbed by them, and
slowly, they become your everything.
And the danger of course in loving someone too much ...
in losing yourself so completely within someone else that you
can no longer exist without them ...
is that the moment you lose that person ...
you lose *everything*.

FATE OR FAILURE?

Sometimes I wonder if we made a mistake.
What if we weren't supposed to let each other go?
What if it was a test ... and we failed?

'TU ME MANQUES'

They say that in French there is no literal translation for
'I miss you', and that instead they say *'tu me manques'*, which
has a meaning more akin to *'You are missing from me'*.
And is that not the most apt description of losing somebody?
Because if you miss a person, you wish they were there with you
– but if a person is missing, then something is deeply wrong
because they are not where they are supposed to be.
So when I say that I miss you, what I really mean is the French
version, because I do not simply wish you were here – you are
missing *from* me.
There is a hole where you used to be and I am incomplete
because of it.
My world is no longer right because you are meant to be here
and you're not.

A WORDS TRUE MEANING

It's funny how we say a person 'made' us when they actually
broke us.
Sort of like how I say 'funny'... but I actually mean sad.

THE BROWN PALING FENCE

I was just the boring, brown paling fence nobody ever noticed,
and you were the ivy that needed something to cling to.
You grew on me a little at first, and then you took over so quickly
that before I realised it you were everywhere, in every crack and
crevice of me.

At first I thought I was better off with you; I wasn't boring and
brown anymore, I was alive and green.
I thought you were better off with me too, because I lifted you up
and encouraged you to grow.
I didn't constantly cut you down and make you crawl along the
ground like your so-called caretaker always did.

But perhaps it wasn't as symbiotic as I'd first thought.
I *felt* completed by you, as you crawled into every crack and
crevice of me … but maybe you weakened me.
Maybe underneath it all, you undermined my foundations and
made all those little cracks bigger.

Perhaps that is why – when you were ripped away from me
– I was left broken, unable to stand alone …
and completely fell apart.

SHIPS IN THE NIGHT

We were, as they say, like ships in the night ... so close yet so far, and all of that. And so there was nothing I could do but watch helplessly as you drifted away from me, powerless to change the tides.
And now I am an empty vessel, aimlessly drifting with no will to weather the storms.
I am a ghostly ship, battered and damaged, doomed to sail the seas alone forever ...
For you were my guiding light,
my north star,
my compass and all my maps.
Without you I am directionless, lost ...
and fearful I am going in circles.

EMPTINESS

You'll never know how much emptiness can hurt; how the weight
of it can crush you or how a hand can ache without another to
hold it.
You'll never know how big an empty bed can be when you sleep
in it alone, or just how long the days can feel when they have no
purpose left in them.
You'll never know just how hollow laughter can sound when it's
holding back tears, or how vacant eyes can look in a mirror when
you hate what you see.
You'll never know how it feels to be incomplete because you gave
your heart to somebody who left you with nothing but an empty
chest and a head full of memories you can't erase.

So don't tell me you're sorry for the pain you've caused when you
don't even know what it feels like.
You can keep your empty apology.
You've given me enough emptiness already.

TAINTED MEMORIES

You've tainted every memory I have.
No matter what I remember – I remember you.
It doesn't matter how far back I go, you're there.
Even in my childhood memories I remember you, and not
because you were there at the time, but because they're memories
I've shared with you or they're memories that remind me of a
feeling you once gave me.

There is no part of me you haven't touched.
Every place I go I think of you, even the places I've never been to
with you, because at some point I've been there and I've thought
of you.
You're everywhere … and it's killing me.
You're in my head.
You're in my heart.

And I can't get you out.

'GOODBYE'

What is it like to have such power over another human being?
To walk into someone's life and change it completely.
To redefine everything they thought they knew about love and
then walk away completely unscathed.

What must that be like?
To have the power to completely destroy a person with a single
word.

NO ANSWER

It's nearly 10pm on a Saturday night and all I have on my mind
are endless questions.
Where are you right now in this moment?
Are you happy?
Are you lonely?
How was your day?
Did anything funny happen?
Did you think of me today?
Will you think of me tomorrow?
Do you ever lie in bed and look at the empty pillow on the other
side and try to imagine me there like I do with you? I know you
used to, you told me so ... but do you still do it?
Do you imagine me opening my eyes and smiling at you?
Because that's what I picture when I imagine you.
Sometimes I even smile back at the empty space ... just a little.
Do you ever just think thoughts to me?
Ask me questions in your mind like I'm doing right now?
It's like I'm trying to call you on an imaginary phone in my head.
But there's no answer.

THE LAST TIME

The last time I felt alive
I was looking into your eyes,
breathing your air,
touching your skin,
saying goodbye.

The last time I felt alive ...
I was dying.

THE DEPTHS

I was always so cautious.
But you ... you just dived headfirst into everything.
You dived into my life and made waves.
Then you left me alone ... and I couldn't swim.

I couldn't swim.

THE FAULT LIES WITHIN

I don't know why I let myself believe we would be in each other's lives forever ... in retrospect, it was such a childish notion.
I don't know how I ever thought it would work, I just did. I simply believed that somehow everything would work itself out and we'd be in each other's lives forever.
I suppose it was because you were such a unique and irreplaceable person.
I knew I would never stop loving you and would certainly never want you out of my life, and being the person that I am, I couldn't imagine ever hurting you or doing anything to make you want to leave.
In my mind it seemed reasonable to think something so amazing could last indefinitely.
So I let myself hope ... I allowed myself to dream.
I gave myself permission to believe in something that felt certain, but in reality it could never have worked and was doomed to fail from the start.
So when the reality of the situation finally tripped me up and I fell down, I had only myself to blame because I should have known better.
Life is not a fairytale with happily ever afters.
And as simple as love can be – and it really was so easy with you – life is what's complicated, and I think perhaps it was more convenient to forget that for a while. To pretend things could have been different ... that this was that one special time when all my bad luck would finally balance out and everything would go right for me.
I made a decision with my heart, and the heart loves to ignore facts it doesn't want to acknowledge because they ruin the dream.
And the sad fact is that the dream is now gone and I have no one to blame for this emptiness but myself.

CRASH HARD

It's terrifying how your life changes without your consent.
You meet someone one day and before you realise it's happening,
you're falling in love with them, and it's too late to stop.
It's like that reoccurring dream where you're driving towards a
red light and suddenly the brakes don't work.
It's terror in slow motion.
You're drifting … drifting towards the intersection with your foot
to the floor so hard that you're practically standing and there's
nothing you can do to stop it.
It's out of your control; you know you're going to crash so hard
it's going to kill you.

But just before that inevitable moment, you wake up and you feel
relieved.
It's okay; it was just a bad dream.
You're in love and everything's okay.
So you walk around in your half-dream state, blissfully
unaware you're still asleep, until the point that you wake up for
real one day to the realisation that the person you love is gone.
And there you are, sobbing like a two year old because you didn't
ask for this. This isn't fair.
This isn't right.
You saw the red light ahead … and you tried so hard to put the
brakes on.

MEANINGLESS WORDS

We used to be something real, but now we're just words.
Words in my memory, words in old letters and emails …
and words that were left unsaid.
They're so empty, aren't they – words.
They're just sounds you make that have a recognised meaning
to somebody else, almost like crying in a way …
But if no one's around to hear them, does that make them
meaningless?
If I called you and told you that I loved you, would it mean
something to you? Would it make a difference?
Or is it better to keep those words purely as silent thoughts
and nothing more?
Is it the act of speaking them aloud or writing them out for
someone else to acknowledge that gives them their meaning?
Or does their existence alone give them substance, even if
they're only thoughts?
You know, so much time has passed now that your name has
become just a word. It is no longer a greeting, a loving
description or a passionate whisper.
It has lost those meanings.
So tell me, if I never speak your name again … will you
eventually mean nothing to me?

ALL THE LITTLE PIECES OF YOU

I love them you know ... all the little pieces of you.

But sometimes I wish I could say that I'd gathered them up, torn
them all into tiny little pieces and blew them into the wind.
Not because I'm angry or hateful towards you ... nothing even
close to that.
It is simply because I wish I could say I was free of them.
I wish I could say I was liberated from this feeling I carry with me
all the time -this heartfull melancholy.
I wish I could say that I'd cried my last tears for you, opened my
hands to the sky and let it all go.

But I can't.
Because every day I take them all - all those little pieces of you -
and I try so desperately to stick them back together, trying to
make something tangible out of the nothing that's left.

You know I love them ... all the little pieces of you.

That's why I can't let them go.

LOST DREAMS

The times your absence hurts the most is when I wake up
knowing I have dreamt of you but cannot remember the dream.
Like a person groping in the dark for a light switch, I try
frantically to reach for some recollection to bring the memory
back.
I try to recall even the slightest detail ... where we were, what
happened between us, even a single word you spoke to me –
anything to pull the recollection of you back before it fades away
completely.
But it is always in vain, and I am never able to grasp the
fragments before they fall away and out of my reach forever.
It always feels as though I have been robbed of you ... as though
you were here in the room with me only moments ago and the
memories of it have been stolen from me.

Perhaps you were here.
Perhaps we are together in our dreams and the moment we wake
is the moment you leave,
and as always, when you leave ...
you take my dreams with you.

WE USED TO BE SO CLOSE

You and I used to be about as close as two people could possibly
be, and now look at us … so alienated … so separate.
I remember a time when we used to work like a well-oiled
machine – all the intricate thoughts and emotions between us
moving through rhythmic motions in perfect harmony.
Whatever happened to those days when we were so in tune that
we could sense even the slightest emotional tremors in each other
without even having to be in the same room?
The way we would reach out to one another with our thoughts
and listen with our hearts, always wanting to be closer, ever
closer …
Where did that all go?

What a sad, sorry thing it is now. All that we had is gone, left
abandoned as though it were a room and you simply got up one
day and left.
But my love still lingers in the doorway looking back, refusing to
leave because it is unable to accept the emptiness you've left in
your wake.

And all I am left with is that thought – that single sentence
echoing around in my head …
'We used to be so close.'
What a sad, sorry sentence that is.
Is anything more expressive of emptiness than that?
Six little words that say so much about just how little is left.

METAPHORICAL SIDEWALK

I am walking on a metaphorical sidewalk, swept along amongst a crowd of imaginary people bustling to get to wherever it is they're going in life.
But I'm not like them. I don't walk at the same pace.
I am aimless, partly because I have no destination and partly because I'm so tired.
I'm tired of purposely walking at an insane pace with no real purpose; call me crazy but it feels insane to me!?!
So I stop – in the middle of the sidewalk.

I stand, completely still.

Nobody notices.
Nobody stops.
Like ants with a tiny rock in their path, they detour around me, swarming to the left and to the right.
People coming the opposite way stare ahead with their determined stares, and I just stand there wanting to cry like a lost child in a shopping mall.
But that's how life is.
It waits for no one.
It pushes on like that man in a suit or that kid with a backpack on, or any one of the hundreds of faces that form the blurring mass that passes me by.
I am not big enough to stop the tide, no one is.
I am but one tiny rock in the path of an ant swarm.
I am one person standing still on a metaphorical sidewalk amongst a crowd of imaginary people, desperately wishing that time itself will stop – flicker momentarily like a florescent bulb when it is switched on – and then ... wind backwards.
People walking, people talking – backwards.
Streams of strangers walking backward towards me, dissecting into two streams to my left and my right – backwards.

Determined faces getting further away, replaced by other determined faces until the moment I feel fingers interlock with mine.
Someone takes my hand.
I look up and you are beside me once more, holding my hand.
It is all undone.
You have not let go; you are still with me.
The sea of strangers fades from my awareness.
I can see only you.

Life nowadays feels very much like a sea of strangers passing me by on a metaphorical sidewalk.
But it can never go backwards ... and as much as I wish standing still will let me see your face again, it won't.
You walked on ahead of me a long time ago.
You are now just another imaginary stranger with a determined face and a purposeful, energetic walk hidden amongst the crowd.

I am the only one standing still.

RECREATION

It is the subtleties of a person that you miss the most.
The same basic personality traits and grander gestures can be
found in other people, but it's those tiny, subtle nuances you miss
because they cannot be replicated or impersonated by anyone
else.
It's those things you miss but cannot define or articulate: minute
body language traits, the slightest difference between 134
different smiles, each meaning something different, an
encyclopaedia of knowledge that comes from the intimate study
of another human being.
And the worst thing is that they're the things you can't write, you
can't compose, you can't draw.
You cannot recreate a person no matter how hard you try.
I think that's why we write, or paint or play music.
Why we search for quotes on love, but as much as they move us
they never seem to sum up the person we lost or the way they
make us feel ... it's because we want that person back
so desperately.
More than that, we want them back in a format that is ours and
that we can control.
Because a painting, a symphony or a poem lives forever ...
and more importantly, it cannot ever leave.

A MOMENT IN TIME

Sometimes I wish you could have lived a single moment as me.
That somehow there was a way you could have experienced a
single second of time from inside my mind and felt what I felt
when I looked at you.
But what moment would I have chosen?
Would it be the feeling I would get whenever I hadn't seen you
in a while?
That first instant I would see you standing on the street and
my heart would jolt inside my chest and my breath would
catch in my throat.
The way it felt like a sunrise in my heart when I would see the
recognition spread across your face, as you would look up at
me and smile.

Or would I have chosen a moment of being separated from
you so you could feel that ache, that longing, that tugging at
my heart ... that NEED to be close to you?

Or would I perhaps have chosen a moment when we were
kissing one-another ... where it was like suddenly being
suspended a thousand feet above the clouds ... no air, no sound
... nothing but you and me frozen in that moment with the rest
of the world somewhere far below.

I so wish you could have felt even a split-second of any one of
those moments as me.
I feel sure that a second would have been all you'd have
needed ...
Because perhaps if you'd *felt* – even for the briefest moment –
just how much I loved you ...
you would never have let me go.

EVER AFTER

Call me a dreamer or an optimist, but I refuse to give up hope
that somewhere out there, there's a place where you and I are
happy together.
I don't know if it's another time or another world, I only know
that there has to exist a place where everything turns out okay
for us.
I have to believe that ... that somewhere out there the universe
gives us our happy ending.

I LOVED YOU

I loved you, you know ... I really did.

I loved you to a point where it completely blinded me – where all I could see and think and feel was you.

I loved you with an intensity that defied description.

I was inexplicably drawn to you, like a wave to the shore – yet I never questioned it.

It felt completely natural, as if it was predestined by some celestial force beyond my understanding or control.

It felt like my entire existence centered around you and was somehow always meant to.

I was drawn to you – not in the way a person is drawn to somebody they admire – but with a deeper force, like a gravitational pull.

Being in your presence was like staring into the sun – you overwhelmed me, you dazzled me ... you blinded me.

And I'll never forget what it felt like to lose you.

To be plunged into a cold, unending darkness without a flicker of hope that you would ever come back.

It felt like the end of the world ...

Like watching the sun set into the distance and knowing it would never rise again.

EXCESS BAGGAGE

I see now that it's never going to get any easier.
It's never going away, this missing you.
It's going to become a sadness I incorporate into myself
– along with all the other sadnesses – and quietly carry around
with me forever.

BROKEN

I gave far too much
for the promise of so little
that ironically ended up
just as broken as I was.

SO THIS IS 'GETTING BETTER'

Sometimes I feel hollow inside, like an empty drum.
I work.
I talk to people.
I laugh.
I do things to keep busy … but it all feels so empty.
It's a purposeless routine; I have no real direction and I can't see my life changing any time soon.
I know this is better than the constant agony I used to feel when you first left, but sometimes I wonder … is this what 'getting better' is?
Is this all it will ever be, this emptiness?
I know you shouldn't believe that a person can complete you, you're supposed to be a complete person on your own and I was, I always have been … but I wasn't a *happy* person.
I just sort of existed and did things because that's what I thought I was supposed to do, but I never felt inspired by anything and I was never really happy until I met you.
And it's hard to let go of that.
It's something so many people take for granted every day, and I absolutely cherished every second of it.
But losing it was hard.

I'm doing my best.
I tell myself, '*Head up, don't cry, look ahead not behind*', but even my own laughter sounds different now … false and hollow as though it's not even mine.
And those are the times it's hardest not to miss you, when I'm smiling or laughing on the outside but feeling so little on the inside.
I ask myself, '*Is this really getting better? Or is this just the numbness you feel when you've felt too much pain for too long?*'

FROM A DISTANCE

Everybody wants their own little place in the world,
and maybe mine is here ...
loving you from a distance.

THE SADDEST TRUTH OF ALL

You can't always be somebody's *'forever'*.
Sometimes you're just their *'summer'* or their *'little while'* …
Sometimes not even that.
Sometimes the closest you'll get is their *'almost'* or their *'maybe'*.
And when they leave, the best you can hope for is to be their
'what if' or *'remember when'* …
Because you can't always be somebody's *'forever'* …
even if they were yours.

BLISSFULLY UNAWARE

I loved you ... without cause, or reason, or doubt.
I loved you to the edge of what my soul could endure, and then
I loved you just a little bit more.
I loved you beyond measure, beyond hope and beyond all sense
of rationality.
I loved you until the light had gone, until the years had gone,
and until my tears had all but drowned me.
I loved you until it ruined me; like an ancient temple I stood,
abandoned and forgotten before finally caving under the sheer
weight of time.
And in the end it changed nothing – all that love.
For here I was, dying for you until my spirit was weary ...
And there you were, living your life ... blissfully unaware.

HURT

It didn't hurt me.
Not '*hurt*'.
Hurt is a four-letter word.
It's short, almost cute sounding.
'*Aawwww, did that hurt?*'
No.
It didn't hurt.
Destroyed, obliterated, desecrated, annihilated, demolished,
shattered, or demoralised maybe …
But no, it didn't hurt me.
It didn't '*hurt*' me at all.

THE SUM OF IT

He said 'I love you'
but he didn't choose me.
I guess the actions had costs
but the words were free.

SILENT WHISPERS

Does her name
… taste the same
as mine, mumbled in the dark?

And do you fear
… that she will hear
its echo in your empty heart?

NO CONTACT

It's painful loving someone from afar, watching them from the outside.
The once familiar elements of their life reduced to nothing more than occasional mentions in conversations and faces changing in photographs.
They exist to you now as nothing more than living proof that something can still hurt you ... with no contact at all.

PAST LOVES

If you have a moment
and are so inclined,
spare a thought for past loves
you've long left behind.

For if you read their thoughts
it might surprise you to find,
just how often
you've been on their mind.

THE OTHER SIDE

I suppose I could turn around and walk away too …
But secretly, it would only ever be in the hope that one day, we'll
have walked around the earth and would meet again, somewhere
on the other side.

A PICTURE SPEAKS A THOUSAND WORDS

I saw a picture of you – it was taken within the last few days.
You looked good; you looked happy.

They say a picture speaks a thousand words and this photograph
of you did.
It told me I'd done the right thing … that you were happy in your
life and that I don't belong there.
That I never did.
That picture told me you are living in your present and that I am
living in your past.

That picture of you spoke a thousand words to me … and my
name was not amongst them.

I WISH WE COULD PRETEND

I know we're not in each other's lives anymore, but sometimes I wish we could just spend a day together and have everything be like it was.

Is such a thing possible?

To spend a single day in each other's company again, laughing and kissing and talking about everything and nothing.

Would it really be so terrible to meet somewhere and have lunch together and pretend it's the past ... that we're back in time and you're still the one person I can rely on when the whole world is against me?

If I ever asked you, could you do it – pretend that you still care for old times' sake?

It's foolish, I know, which is why I'll never ask.

But the truth is that life's not been easy since you left, and I'd do just about anything right now to be able to pretend just for one day that I'm happy again.

That everything's okay – that everything will be okay – because that's how you always made me feel, even on the worst days imaginable.

But that was the past and I know I live in the here and now.

I need to face reality.

But the reality is that the day you walked out of my life, I lost the greatest thing I ever had and it's been nothing but losses ever since.

IF WISHES WERE HORSES

I wish you were here but you're not.
I wish you'd come back but you won't.
I wish things had of been different but they aren't.
I wish I meant as much to you as you do to me ... but I don't.
And if wishes were horses, I'd have enough to build a merry-go-round, so my thoughts of you could go round and round in circles forever with me always chasing you, but never catching up.
I'd chase you forever you know ... even though I know I'd never get close.

MY SECRET

After all this time,
you're still my secret.

After all this time,
the parts I hide from him
still belong to you.

HAPPY YOU'RE HAPPY

I'm happy that you're happy … really I am.
You've moved on with your life and things are falling into place
for you.
And even though it meant letting me go in the process, I'm glad
you found happiness.

Sometimes I even have moments in my own life where I'm
happy too …

But it doesn't mean I don't still wish things were different.

It doesn't mean I don't wish we could have been happy together.

REGRESSION

Sometimes I still get these urges to contact you.
It feels like pure desperation ... like my skin is crawling and my
eyes are burning and I just want you back in my life so badly!
And I don't know why or where these sudden urges come from.

Why do I still do this, even after all this time?
It's like I'm getting out, I'm almost clear ... and then suddenly
I feel like I would do absolutely anything just to have you back
in my life again.
Even for a single moment ... just to see you, talk to you
– *anything!*
It's like I don't *want* to be out.
I still want to be in love with you, because in my mind, loving
you equates to happiness and I just want that back ... just for
one second.

But I have to remind myself it's not healthy.
Loving you is not like it used to be – it's not real anymore.
It's not happy, it's not positive ... and it's gone and I can't go
back.
All I can do is put the phone down, blink back the tears ...
and keep moving forward.

I STAND ALONE

These last few days have been difficult and I've wanted so much
to contact you.
I haven't, of course, because I know that I can't, but that old
familiar feeling is there and I've had to fight so hard not to give
in to it.
I suppose it's only natural in times like these ... when the ground
feels like it's crumbling under my feet, it makes sense that all
I want to do is run back to the last solid stable thing I can
remember.
There's so much going on and so much going wrong ... and as
always you're the only one I want to turn to.
But I remind myself that it's not an option anymore, no matter
how difficult life gets.
You are no longer a part of my life.
So no matter how frightened I am or how much it feels like the
whole world is crumbling away beneath my feet – I cannot run
to you.
You are no longer my safe place, my confidant or my salvation.
I must learn to stand on my own two feet again.

WE DON'T TALK ANYMORE

We haven't seen or spoken to each other in the longest time.
In fact, we live almost completely separate lives now, except for
where the outer parts of our social circles overlap.
And though we may not hear *from* each other anymore, we do
still hear *about* each other from time to time.
I often wonder what happens when you hear my name.
Do you feel even one of the plethora of emotions I experience
whenever somebody talks about you?
Or is it just me, because I was never able to let go?
We may be distant enough that we don't run into each other, but
we're not so far apart that we couldn't reach out to one another ...
if we really wanted to.
But we don't, and that's what says it all really – isn't it.
We don't contact each other ... we stay right where we are, each
within the confines of our own little circle, never crossing that
imaginary line.
And the funny thing is that despite the fact we have different
feelings towards the current situation, we both keep things the
way that they are for the same reason: because you're happy with
your life the way it is.

MY FAVOURITE SONG

Meeting you was not so much like getting to know you as it was
like listening to a tune you don't remember hearing before, yet
you always seem to know what the next note will be.
You were a familiar melody – so addictive that before I realised it
you were stuck in my head and I couldn't get you out.
Every moment of you played on constant repeat and would go
round in my head for hours.
Slowly you became the soundtrack to my life; every place I went,
every person I spoke to, every dream I dreamed – there you were,
constantly playing in the background.
For whatever reason you resonated with me like no one else ever
had, and I listened to you intently ... studied you and replayed
you until I had memorised you perfectly.

Then you pressed the stop button one day and I didn't hear
anything from you for a long time.
The sudden silence was painful and lonely, so I kept replaying
you in my mind to keep me company, over and over until I
thought I'd go insane.
Eventually I tried to fade you out in the hopes that I'd forget you,
and I'll admit that you are quieter now.
I suppose it's only natural that the more distance there is between
us the quieter you become, and the more time that goes by the
more our conversations fade away like echoes.

But you were like my favourite song once ... and lately, I'm
forgetting all the words and I don't know how to feel about it.
But the one thing I do know for certain is that somehow I had
known you long before I knew you.

That is why you were already so familiar to me, and that is how I know that even if you were to fade to a mere whisper, it would only take a single moment with you for everything to come flooding back to me once again.

And as much as I miss the sound of your voice … I know that wall of silence is the only thing keeping the emotions at bay.

AN UNREQUITED ROMANCE

I believed them when they said that missing someone takes the
place of loving them ...
That longing is what you hold onto in the night to keep warm and
that memory becomes your lover.
But once I'd lost myself to the utter despair that missing you
brought me, all I could feel was just how cold and empty longing
was.
And as the memories started to leave me – just as you had done –
I began to realise that this too was an unrequited romance.

HOMESICK

Your memory feels like home to me.
So whenever my mind wanders, it always finds its way back
to you.

PRESERVATION

After you had gone, it began to feel as though you had died ...
strange to say it, but it's true.
And I thought about having a funeral of sorts – putting
everything to do with you in a box and burying it – but even the
mere thought of doing that made me so beside myself with
anguish that I knew I could never go through with it.
And I wondered how we do it for real – put people we love in the
ground – and I realised that we're not really given a choice.
It's taken out of our hands by people who seem to know what to
do in such situations, and before we know it we're watching a
coffin go down.
But that's the difference when you have a choice: I will never
wilfully bury you. You are the one truly good thing in this world.
Sometimes I think that the only thing that allows me to survive in
it at all is the knowledge that you are in it; that somewhere out
there you still exist and as long as that is true then the world is
not so dark ... even if I can't see you.
That thought has kept me going for a long time now.
It's the only ray of hope I have ... you can't ask me to bury that.

HOLDING A CANDLE

I think perhaps I will always hold a candle for you – even until it burns my hand.
And when the light has long since gone, I will be there in the darkness holding what remains, quite simply because I cannot let go.

EVERY TIME YOU LEAVE

This is the nature of us.
I give myself to you – not willingly but as part of a predestined
fate I have no control over.
I cannot explain to you the how or the why ... only that I was
always meant to love you.
And every time you leave, you take a piece of me with you
– a little piece of myself I will never get back.
And I think that is the greatest tragedy of us ... that every time
you go, it hurts a little less ...
Because every time you come back, I give you another little piece
of myself.
And every time you leave again ... there's less of me left to feel
the loss.

YOU'VE HURT ME TOO MUCH

Sometimes you can love somebody with all of your heart and at the same time NOT want them back.

Everything has a breaking point – hearts included – and when it comes to broken hearts, there's only so many times you can piece yourself back together before you realise that you can't go through it any more.

You continue to love them, despite all of their flaws and the pain they've caused you, but you don't want them back because you realise deep down there's no such thing as back.

Not back in time to undo everything that was said and done ...

And not back together again because you're not the same person anymore.

You've been hurt so many times now that you'd rather break your own heart missing them than give them the opportunity to do it again.

CLOSURE

Stop looking for closure because there is no such thing.
In love there is always an exchange – a process of transference
– and it cannot all go neatly back to the way it was before.
You cannot decide which pieces of yourself you keep and which
pieces of another you give back.
Closure … what a misguided dream that is.
You cannot get closure from someone you've loved; they are not
a wound or a door or a chapter in a book.
Relationships are fluid; souls are like water and the love you feel
for them is an ocean.
If the Indian Sea and the Southern Ocean decided to part, how
could they possibly separate from one another?
How could they possibly know which drops of water belonged
to which.

MEMORY BURN

My skin is no longer the same skin that once felt your touch,
but it aches for you all the same.
Recollections of your fingertips have formed their own cellular
memory, and as old cells die, new ones take their place and learn
from them that same painful longing.
I do not know if I would liken you to a tattoo or a scar …
I simply know you can never be erased.

THE ONE

Deep down, I think everybody wants to be 'the one' to someone.
I don't know if I've ever been that person to anyone else, but I do
know you are that person to me.
You are the one.
The only one.

And you always will be.

to my dearest love my brilliant sun,
the world has decided we an no longer be one
so you take the day and ill take the night

you with your happy glow me with my cold lonely light
it must be this way always and forever

they say we can no longer share the sky together
but my nights will follow your brilliant days

i am right behind you and i will love you always
so do not be sad my love those do not yet

for my reason to rise is in watching you set
so never forget that there once was a time

when i truly was yours and you truly were mine
that there once was a moment when i felt you lips

if ever you miss me remember our eclipse

CHAPTER 3
FIRST LIGHT

'It's difficult for me to imagine the rest of my life without you.
But I suppose I don't have to imagine it …
I just have to live it.'

TIME TO GET UP

Sometimes I wonder if our whole relationship was nothing more than a dream I had once.

A dream so pleasant that waking up from it felt painfully jarring, like being taken from a warm comforting bed and plunged into a bath of ice.

Perhaps that is all it ever was... one of those dreams where months go by, but in reality, it lasts only minutes.

It would be so easy to give up living in exchange for sleeping, and I'll admit that for a while I did.

And still there are days I wish nothing more than to fall back asleep, compelled by the thought that I could live a lifetime with you, if I only close my eyes and dream it.

But it's time for me to get up now ...

I have been asleep far too long and there's still so much living left to do.

LOVE OF A LIFETIME

I cannot take back all the minutes, hours and days I spent loving you, and nor would I if I could.

It is not the *taking* back I want so much as the *getting* back.

There is nothing I would not give for one more second, one more moment … one more chance.

But in truth, I know it would make no difference – even if I had a million years –because I would never be done loving you.

I would always feel as though it ended too soon and I still have so much love to give.

So go out into the world and be happy.

Know that you are someone special who changed the course of a life with both your presence and your absence, and that I will spend every one of my remaining weeks, months and years missing you.

Because whether you realise it or not – every moment of my lifetime has been dedicated to loving you …

even if you don't want to spend it with me.

A HIDDEN BLESSING

There is a hidden blessing in knowing something will end before
it has even begun.
It is in the way cut flowers are doomed to die but they still light
up a room just the same.
It is the reason we embark upon a journey when we know that
eventually, we must always return home.
And it was in the way I cherished every second I spent with you.
It is a bittersweet truth that our life experiences have deeper
meaning and are profoundly more beautiful when we know they
will not last.
So if I can find a quiet peace in anything, it is that I never took
you for granted.
I felt blessed for every moment you were in my life, every kind
word you ever spoke, every laugh or smile you gifted upon me.
I was grateful for you, from the day you entered my life – through
to the day you left it …

I still am.

A STEP (IN THE RIGHT DIRECTION)

Lately my hands feel a little emptier, as if they no longer know
what they are for or what they should do.
At least I think it's my hands – it's hard to know quite where this
listlessness comes from at times.
And I know I'll find things to fill the emptiness; people will love
me and I'll love them.
I'll make things and I'll be somebody and I'll have thank yous
and applause.
But it'll never be the same – because nothing can replace you.

But I'll always wonder about you; I'll wonder where you are, if
you're happy and if you're somebody special to someone.
I'll wonder what you have to fill your emptiness with ... and if,
in the end, it was worth leaving me behind for.
I sincerely hope it was.

LETTING YOU GO

It's alright to go out into the world and live your life without me.
You exist ... and that is enough for me.
I don't need to see you or touch you or hold you.
I don't need to feel your kiss, or see your eyes light up when you
smile, or hear your laughter in my ears.
For I have had all those things once ... and that is enough.
To know that you exist is enough.
Your happiness is mine and if that means that I never spend
another moment in your presence and the thought of me never
crosses your mind, then I guess this is what you call 'acceptance'.
This is that moment when I open my hands to the sky and give
you to the world. You cannot own a person ... and love is a gift
given freely with no guarantee of return.
That is its most beautiful aspect ... its purity; that it exists
individually, irrespective of reciprocation.
For you are you, and I am I, and once we were we ... but as long
as I exist and so do you – know that I will always love you.

THE BUTTERFLY EFFECT

We are always so blissfully unaware of our own fate.
We never seem to realise that at any given time, we could be in a
moment that is triggering unforeseeable circumstances that will
end up changing our lives forever.
Like meeting new people ... I do it all the time and think nothing
of it.
A look, a smile, a conversation ...
How was I to know that *this* person would be different?
That *this* was the moment where my life would change forever?
Perhaps it was the butterflies in my stomach ... maybe that's what
should have told me that this would one day become the point
where 'before' and 'after' would forever be defined.

But how was I to know what the aftermath would be?
How was I to know that a tsunami of pain was about to hit me
completely unaware?
How could I have foreseen that the butterfly effect of this one
conversation would eventually lead to my complete and utter
destruction?
It's cruel that we don't get to choose who we love ... it's like a
train wreck we never see coming.
But the funny thing is ...
if you *gave* me the choice ...
if I'd somehow known ahead of time just how broken this person
would leave me and had the choice between walking into my fate
knowingly – or walking away before it even began ...
I could not say I would have chosen any different.

CROSSING PATHS

The universe works in mysterious ways, and just as the heavens
shift so that certain planets may briefly align only once in a
lifetime – so too can this happen with souls.

Sometimes you will meet someone who seems so perfect for you
that it is as if you were created from the same celestial material ...
yet you find your trajectories taking you away from each other in
hopelessly opposite directions.

It seems almost cruel ... to find a love so perfect, only to lose it
after such a brief time.

Understand that this is simply because your paths were destined
to cross, but not converge as one.

You are, to each other, but a shooting star ... a momentary flash of
brilliance ... a beacon of light sent to brighten each other's lives
and illuminate each other's true path.

So let them go with a thankful heart.

Wish them well on their journey and accept with grace the fact
that some people fit perfectly into your heart but not your life,
and it is as simple and as complicated as that.

CARPE DIEM

Loving you was always something of an extreme sport – a sort of self-destructive thrill seeking behaviour I found terrifying, yet strangely addictive.
The highs were unlike anything I'd ever felt: the happiness, the excitement and the laughter were all so intense.
Being with you was like every happy moment I'd ever had combined into one feeling and magnified a thousand times over.
But the lows are worse when you compare them to a high like that … and they didn't just come at the end.
I can remember there were times when it hurt to love you …
a painful sadness that came from knowing that nothing lasts forever.

But still I dared to hope.
And it is a frightening thing – to hope.
To wish for something you know can never be a reality.
That's what loving you was like … like jumping out of a plane without a parachute and thinking, *'Maybe I'll be lucky and have a soft landing'*, but knowing full well it was probably going to be the end of me.
But I did it anyway.
I jumped right in – knowing the consequences – but despite it all, I wouldn't take it back even though it ultimately destroyed me.
Because until I'd met you, I'd always felt as though I merely 'existed', and even though a part of me died the day I lost you, I still believe that being with you was worth it because when I think back on the time we spent together …
I know I lived every moment.

GLIMPSES

Not everything our eyes are drawn to can stay in our sights
forever.
Not everything our hands reach for can be ours to hold for a
lifetime.
Sometimes we're allowed glimpses of things ... worlds we cannot
be a part of or things we love but cannot keep.
Understand that this is not a punishment.
It's not that we haven't earned happiness or that we don't deserve
it – it is simply because some happiness is transient and cannot
stay with us forever.

But what defines us as the person we are is how we accept our
fate and how gracefully we let go of those things we wish to love
forever, but cannot hold onto.
It's not easy – I won't tell you it is because it's not ... but
somehow it feels 'right'.
I cannot explain it any other way than that, just that you will
come to an understanding that as painful as it is – this is the way
things are meant to be.

But the choice of how we move forward from this loss is ours and
ours alone.
We can choose to be bitter over the injustice of being unable to
possess the happiness we desire – or we can choose to carry a
piece of that happiness with us, simply by being grateful that we
were lucky enough to know happiness ... to call it by its name
and say that it was ours for the brief time we had it.

Because as much as it hurts to let go of something like that, it's
nothing compared to the lifetime of emptiness we would have
lived without it.

LOVING A BROKEN PERSON

It takes someone special to love a person who's broken –
someone who's willing to look past all the cracks and fault lines
to see the person the fragments form in their entirety.
It takes someone with patience and a gentle spirit ... someone
who realises that broken people may appear sharp and hostile,
but they are in fact fragile and need to be treated with care.
But most of all, it takes someone who's brave to love a person
who's broken, because they will hurt you – even if they don't
mean to.
There will be times you will try to hold them, but they'll be too
afraid to let you close.
Their words will be the weapons they use to push you away, and
they'll sting you like splinters and get under your skin.
But if you are brave enough to try ...
To try *again* ...
To keep trying until you break through those defences ...
You will find that a broken person will love you unlike anyone
else ever has.
Every fractured part of their personality will love you and reflect
your love back at you a thousandfold.
They'll make you laugh, they'll make you cry, they'll be the
biggest roller-coaster of emotions you'll ever know ... but they'll
be worth it ... so very worth it, because their trust is worth its
weight in gold.
And with every part of themselves they uncover for you comes
the knowledge that you are special; that you are their only one;
that you are an explorer in an uncharted wilderness seeing a
hidden treasure that nobody else has ever gotten close enough to
see ... that jewel of a smile that shines only for you.

DESPITE OUR OUTCOME
THIS WILL ALWAYS BE TRUE

Getting to know you was the most wonderful adventure.
It was like suddenly discovering the love of my life and my best
friend all in one. There were moments when I was almost afraid
that this couldn't be real … that *you* couldn't be real.
Everything about you was just too perfect and we were so
compatible it just didn't seem possible.
But I surrendered to the feeling … let it take me where I knew I
was fated to go, and I'm so glad that I did because it allowed me
to get to know you, and in getting to know you I was getting to
know myself because YOU are the other half of me.
It was discovering new things about myself I never knew, and
remembering things about myself I thought I'd lost like my
childlike joy and ability to laugh loudly and love deeply.
Finding you brought a magic and a joy into my life unlike
anything I have ever known and there is not a day that goes by
when I am not grateful that on a planet of over seven billion
people, I was lucky enough to find you.

whenever people look at me, they see different things depending on
who they are. they see a family member or
an employee... a potential customer or a face in a crowd but whenever
you looked at me, i always knew that somehow you were seeing 'me' and that is
what i loved about you the ... you were the only person who
looked past every mask i ... and looked directly at 'me'. it
didn't matter how much i tried to hide you
always ... the real me beneath everything else past as i ... the real
you and that is ... what i will always miss about you the most...
because that is ... what i know i will
never find ... somebody else

ADDENDUM

'You left me wanting.
And though I gave up waiting …
I'll never stop wishing.'

A CHOICE

After you left, I found myself lost in a kind of perpetual darkness.
It seemed almost to be a never ending night, devoid of any kind
of hope or light …
and it was the longest night of my life.

But eventually, there came a point when I realised I had a choice:
either close my heart forever or keep it open despite the pain.
And I'll admit that it was tempting … to cry *'close the gates'* and
shut the whole world out behind walls and doors again.
But I didn't.
I left myself open and instead I let the whole world in.

Sometimes there's so much pain I can hardly bear it.
I feel like I can't possibly give any more of myself.
That I am spent …
tired of caring,
tired of hurting,
tired of writing out my vulnerabilities and putting them on
display.
But every time someone says thank you for helping me heal,
thank you for your words,
thank you for being my voice when no one else understood,
I realise that this is my purpose now.

You know, there once was a time when all the love I had in the
world went to you.
Now all the love I have for you goes out to the world.

INDEX

ABOUT THE AUTHOR

A writer of words, a poetic soul, an emotive expressionist, Ranata Suzuki is an anonymous writer based in Sydney, Australia.

Known only by her avatar of a bird carrying a book, for years she has touched the hearts and minds of people across the globe with her words, sharing excerpts from her personal journal in the form of poetry and quotations on social media.

The publication of The Longest Night marks her long-awaited debut poetry collection, which is set to enthral both avid fans and new readers alike with its heartfelt sincerity covering the all too relatable themes of heartbreak and loss. Always emotive and spoken with raw honesty, her voice will move you quite simply because it sounds so much like the voice inside your own heart.

"Everybody wants their own little place in the world, and maybe mine is here ... loving you from a distance."

Heartbreak and grief touch every soul at least once in a lifetime and Ranata Suzuki translates those raw emotions into words. The Longest Night combines strikingly poignant quotations, powerfully emotive poetry and captivating silhouette imagery to form a mournful lover's journal that explores a side of love that is deep, dark and hauntingly beautiful.

A book for anyone who has found themselves separated from someone they love no matter the circumstance, The Longest Night is a companion for the broken heart on the painful emotional journey that is losing someone you love from your life.

Its words serve as a comforting reminder, whether you are travelling this road or have recently completed this journey yourself, that despite the loneliness you may sometimes feel along the way none of us walk this path alone.

ISBN 978-0-646-98740-8

90000

9 780646 987408

101 Amazing
Mythical Beasts
and legendary creatures

Jack Goldstein